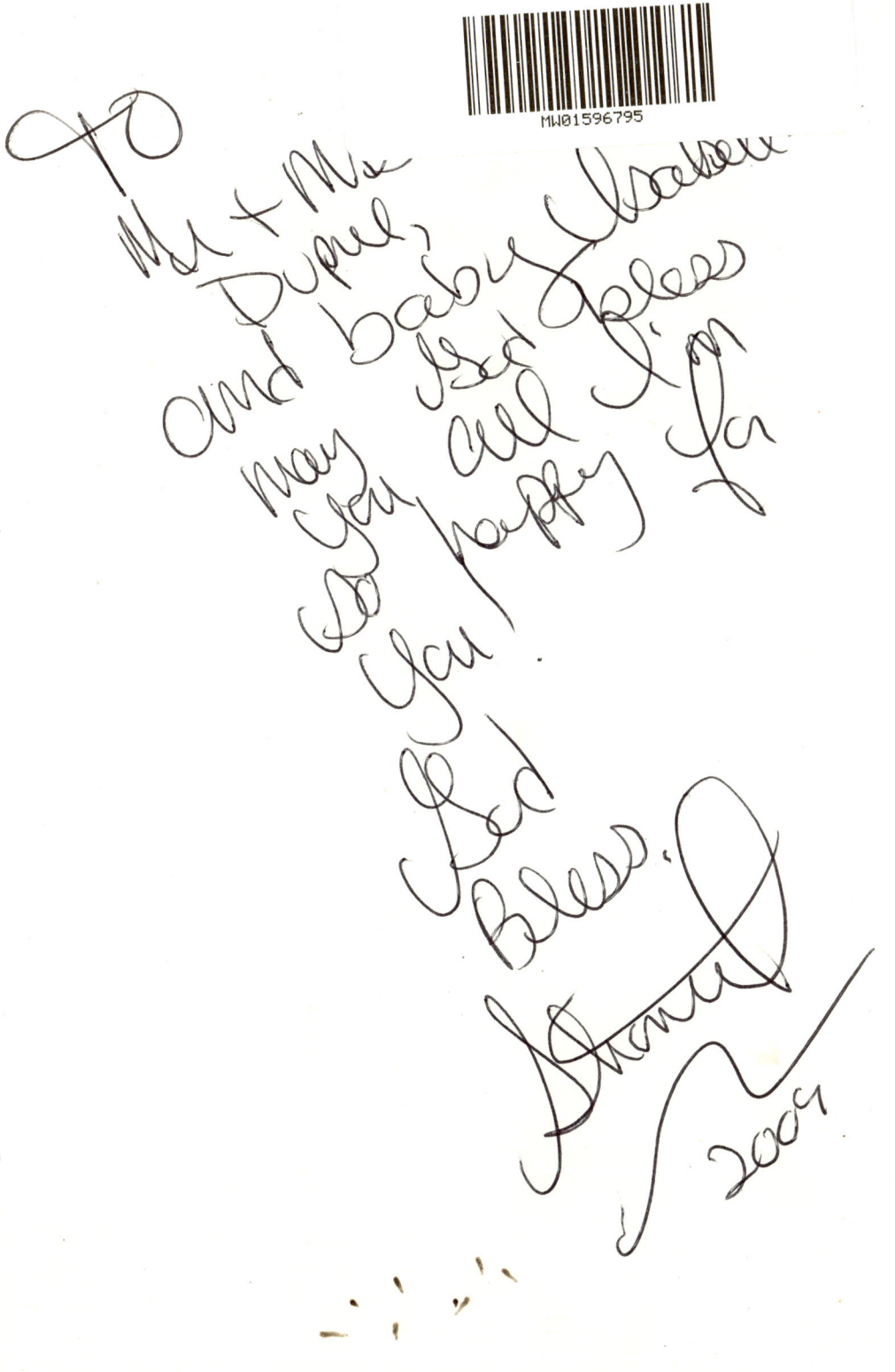

I'm Still Standing

Shontel D. Hightower

authorHOUSE®

AuthorHouse™
1663 Liberty Drive, Suite 200
Bloomington, IN 47403
www.authorhouse.com
Phone: 1-800-839-8640

First published by AuthorHouse 4/2/2009

ISBN: 978-1-4389-5323-6 (sc)

Printed in the United States of America
Bloomington, Indiana

This book is printed on acid-free paper.

Table of Contents

Praise Him!

Praise Him!
Praise the Lord today-Praise him for he is your Father.
Praise Him for all that he has done.
Praise him for saving your soul.
Praise him for he is good.
Praise him for he is worthy to be praised!
Praise him with all that you have.
Praise him for things to come.
Praise him for he is the Lamb of God.
Praise him for keeping you
Praise him with your hands
Praise him by stumping your feet
Praise him and open up your mouth
Praise him with your prayer language
Praise him with the tambourine
Praise him with singing
Praise him by living right
Praise Him
I said Praise Him
Praise the Lord today
Praise him for his greatness
Praise him for his Sovereignty
Praise him because-because he is the Great I AM
Praise him for God sits on high and looks down low
Praise him
Praise him for he can dispatch angels on your behalf
Praise him with gladness
Praise him with joy
Praise him with dancing
Praise him with the trumpet
Praise him for the blood that washes like snow
Praise him for the Holy Spirit

Praise him Oh Praise him
Oh Praise him Oh Praise him
For he is God's son Jesus who is the Christ
I said Praise Him!

My Heart

Hey You!
Do you know me?
It's me you been all in my dream.
At first I didn't see your face I just saw a silhouette of you.
But I get excited just by the thought of you.
Can it be God bringing me a man of my dream so I couldn't wait to go to sleep
just to dream again?
The very thing that I've been praying for night after night I tossed and turned wishing I could see your face.

Then to my surprise you came again you and your dark skin the vision started becoming clear!
Oh goodness it's you a sweet heart is what God said.
He loves you.
You are a man after his heart follow the dream and I will make it plane then my heart started to beat again.

I thought I would never feel this way again.
I sit and wonder.
Do you feel my heart like God let me feel yours the tears I've sown was for you?
Just so God could watch over you.
Keep the heart you have its rare bread you are God's seed.
My heart almost exploded did you feel the beat.
Over, and over, and over again.

I prayed for God's man so I hope to see you again I've been looking forward to my dreams feel my heart pound for you.
I will give up my promise just so your heart can keep on beating see you tonight my dark man I look forward to our life plan.

Desire

The desire that we have comes from God.
The desire to be the women that God has called us to be.
The desire will turn into reality walk in it the preacher says.
This is the way come on and follow the Lord he has so much in store.
The flood gate will open so pick up your sword and walk.
Don't look to the left or to the right follow the light.
Discouragement comes but
I promise you he has a will for your life.
Stop trying to fight.

It is written every breath you take is part of the plan-every move you make is ordained by God.
So like I said this is the way walk in it-Hater's will come but that's to be expected.

Get to moving!
The Lord is waiting your destiny lies ahead.
Smile!

God has your back.
All the other stuff you used to do is under the blood so walk my sister.
Step hard!
Your destiny is straight ahead be encouraged.
The desire you have God put it there just for you boo.

God give me rest

God when you give me rest
Please allow me to enjoy
Lord it's rest in you-is what I need
When I inherit my land let's sit back and talk
Rest Jesus is what I'm asking for
A resting place in you
I live life from day to day all I want is a resting place
Mr. Bills call all day long
And I'm tired of the same old song
Rest is what I need
Rest Jesus just to be in your presence
Just to rest in you
You are awesome
It's you I adore
Look upon my heart and you will truly see that I just want to
rest in you
A resting place Jesus
A place where I can sit and talk to you a place Jesus where I
can just walk with you
Yes!
That is it a resting place in you
That's my desire
That's my prayer
God give me rest

Restore Me

I often sit and wonder why my life is the way that it is
I often wonder if I will ever be delivered
I've been through so much in my life I ask myself do you hear me Lord
Do you see my tear?
Do you see my fears?

Was this a set up all that I've endored in my life?
Failed relationships pain, heartache my family has fallen apart
My daddy left home no father figure around
I tried the church thing but people in that building just sit back and judge me
On my past they look at how I dress not realizing this is all I have left
I cry out to you day and night wondering why I always got to fight life brought things I never could imagine

Why God did all of this happen?
So I decided to have another chat with you because I know I'm not just sitting here going through.
So I picked up my bible and said a little prayer and said I need you Father I want to be restored.

I heard a quiet voice say to me.
Open your bible to Psalm 23:3 I sat up and opened my bible gently and you spoke to me.
"He restoreth my soul: he leadeth me in paths of righteousness for his name sake. (KJV) I just sat there and lifted my hands and said thank you Lord I'm starting to believe you understand.
Then you said to me I'm not done talking to you.

Read Psalm 51 start at verse 12
"Restore unto me the joy of thy salvation and uphold me with thy free spirit; Then will I teach transgressors thy ways: and sinners shall be converted unto thee, Deliver me from blood guiltiness', O God thou God of my salvation: and my tongue shall sing a loud thy righteousness (KJV) I thought to myself could this be do you Oh God want to restore me.

Then the quiet voice said yes it is me.
 I said Oh Lord don't stop please continue to talk to me.
He said child I love you so please don't think I would ever let you go.
Don't be discouraged for I am here I love and care about all of your hurts
I see your pain I see the tears don't worry about anything
I got your back and I see all the devils attacks when you go to church don't worry about folks I'll take care of them I need you to come and dine with me.
Because after a while I'll see you in eternity-Oh Father please forgive me I need you to walk with me then the Lord said I heard your prayer I'm here to restore and repair.

So my child don't give up I'll help you through just keep looking up for I know the thoughts I think towards you, saith the Lord, thoughts of peace and not of evil, to give you an expected end Jeremiah 29:11(KJV) So right now today restoration begins.

Forgiveness

Forgiveness has to occur healing has to be we can't ignore the
past but we have to deal with it.
No matter what it happened!
Whether it was mental or physical abuse-healing begins-
healing begins with the blood of Jesus.
No matter what you've been through-prostitution or even
being a thug-you need healing from God above.
No matter what your past life has brought you the word of
God can restore you.
Healing is what this poem is about.
Lets take away all of the doubt God has a plan for you and
me.
To God be the glory.

So during this life trials and tribulations will come.
Your family and friends will disappoint you but just
remember one thing-forgiveness is a matter of the heart.
You will be free I celebrate forgivness-So today your new life
begins.

Free

Do you know you are free?
Free to live free to walk free to talk free
You are free to be real in this life
Walk in forgiveness be free act free live free
Walk in the spirit of God
Walk in the light don't look back at the past look up to God

When he died on the cross your freedom began
don't be down with your face wearing a frown
Be free in Jesus because who the son set free is free indeed
So believe that you are free
Act like you are free
Free of pain free of shame free of bondage
You my sister
Yes you! Guess what?
You are free!

Struggle

What do you struggle for?
Struggle
What is this really about?
Now you struggle to be kept
Struggle to go to work
Struggle to have relationships
You sit in a crowd of people and struggle to fit in
Well I'm here to tell you my friend no more struggling within
You are who you are no running away
The struggle is for your purpose
When you struggle it's not just for you
So as you take the next step and as you sit and think of the struggle that you are in
Don't be discouraged stand up tall and walk through your struggle
You can do it pray through the struggle fast through your struggle
My friend I tell you this the struggle won't last always!
Amen

Dreams

Dreams is how the Lord deals with me he talks to me he walks with me
Dreams is how I see things
Dreams is the way the Father in heaven express him self to me
Dreams of love dreams of things to come

Joseph from the Old Testament was a dreamer and did he go through
God had him assistant to the King Pharroh
Just think if he never dreamed he would have not reached his destiny

Dreams are a wonderful way to communicate with God from above
So today I ask the Lord keep allowing me to dream so tonight when I sleep father please let me dream

I desire to dream of things to come. Lord show me your mysteries of things to come so I can pray
Now I lay me down to sleep Lord Jesus give me a dream of Peace!

Miracles

Miracles that God perform are so awesome.
How he delivers folks out of bondage yes Lord you are a
miracle working God.
How you change and rearrange our lives.
How you can take a caterpillar and turn it into a beautiful
Butterfly
Yes that's a miracle from our God.
Who else would love us so?
No one but a God who specializes in miracles.
Some of us should be dead sleeping in our grave but the Lord
wouldn't let it be so.

He's working out a miracle for you and for me.
The air we breathe the steps that we take each and every day is
a special gift from God up above.
So sit back and allow him to perform a miracle in you.
Sit back and enjoy the best of God wait and anticipate on
what he will have you to do.

Because my friend it's a miracle inside of you.
Be anxious for nothing if you don't see the miracle yet just
wait and see our Father will perform a miracle.
It's destined to be. You are a miracle.

The still small voice

Do you listen to that still small voice?
Are you attentive to its call?
Do you follow the leading of that voice?
It's the voice of the Lord guiding you telling you where to go
that voice so quite at times you want to ignore it at times you
act like you don't hear it. But you know whose voice it is. It is
the voice of the Lord.
That beautiful voice that guides you through life.
Oh my friends thank God for his voice the still small voice is
the leading of the Holy Spirit.

He tells you to go right instead of going left
When it's so much confusion in your life that voice speaks.
My dear friend listen to that voice it will never steer you
wrong.

That voice will have you to worship Oh thank God for the
Holy Spirit. Thank God for that voice if you don't listen to
that voice what shall you do. Put flesh aside and listen to that
voice.
Put flesh aside and obey that voice you are not crazy.
Think it not strange embrace that voice stand strong and
listen to the leading of that voice.
The still small voice is the voice of the Lord.
Don't move to the left or to the right until you hear that still
small voice.

Peace

You are my peace in the midst of the storm.
When life troubles come up against me you give me peace.
God you allow me to walk in peace.
You are peace.

When things don't go the way that they should you give me
peace.
Peace in life is what I seek.
Quietness in you is what I desire.
God you alone are my peace I desire peace I need peace.

Sometimes in order to have peace you have to let folks go.
Which is never easy?
But if you want Shalom you might have to walk alone.

Seek peace and find it.
Guard your heart for it is the thing to do.
Stand strong don't give up.
God desires for you to have his peace.

He died on Calvary for me and for you.
So don't let his dying be in vain.
You are free to have God's peace it's in his word.

Worship

Worship!
Oh God worship I am a worshiper it is part of my being if I
could not worship-I would surely die.
I wake up in the morning to worship.
I worship on my job!
I worship in my car.
I worship Oh God how I worship.

Because I desire something from you
You know my name you know every hair on my head.
You Oh heavenly father designed me to worship.
I'll sing, I'll dance, I'll praise.
But worship is who I really am.
Just to feel your presence just to wave my hand is worship.
Over powered by the Holy Spirit oh how I look forward to it.
Talking to you in my prayer language is how I worship.

My moan and my groan's are a part of my worship.
So yes it's me a worshiper, Oh-Oh-Oh how sweet it is to allow
the Holy Spirit to dwell in me.
So I can worship in spirit and in truth.
The overflow of God is in the worship.
Deliverance is in the worship.
Holiness is in the worship.
I long to worship.

Again I'll say I'm created to worship.
So don't allow a day to go by without true worship.
Worship our Lord for he is God.

Over flow

Overflow is what we desire.
Seek his will and his face and the overflow will come.
I'm not talking about overflow of money, houses, or a car I'm talking about the overflow of God's love.

The overflow that you feel when you are praying and you are seeking the face of God and you feel him pouring the overflow.
When you feel the presence of the Lord dwelling in your being.

Now that's overflow.

Overflow of God's power to break the yoke of bondage that's the flow of God.
So I urge you to allow God to flow.
Allow the Holy Spirit to be able to maneuver in your life.
Let go and let God flow.
He'll take you places you've never seen.
Pray without ceasing so you my friend can get to the overflow.
I need it I got to have the overflow of God's anointing

Father allow me to get the overflow.
Its joy it's peace it's love it's favor when you are in the overflow.
All things will come so relax and watch and feel the flow.
It's like a cool breeze on a spring day.
I feel it God so today I seek your face for the overflow.
Flow God have your way

The overflow of your power
The overflow of your precious love
Now that's overflow

Blessed

How do you know when you are blessed?
How do you feel blessed?
When all chaos is breaking out all around you?
How do you feel when folks say God bless you when you don't
feel blessed.
Well praise the Lord I have news for you.

You are blessed.

During trials and tribulations you are blessed.
Life storms come and go but during it all you are blessed.
If you are breathing you are blessed.
If you woke up in your right mind you are blessed.
If you work with crazy folks on the job you are blessed.
If you are able to give God a hand wave you my friend are
blessed.
If you can feel the breeze outside you are blessed.
If you can read this poem guess what you are blessed.

You are blessed!

If you can say you are a child of God you are blessed.
Take a moment and look in the mirror and tell your self you
are blessed.
If you can't hear but you are able to sign language you are
blessed.
If you have people to love you are blessed.
If you are successfully single you are blessed.
If you still don't think you're blessed.
Well no matter what you think of yourself I got some good
news for you.

You are blessed!

Every where you go the blessings of God go with you.
You are blessed!
So take a moment and give God some praise for allowing you
to be blessed. Thank you Jesus for blessing me.

A love letter to God

This is my love letter to the Lord.
 If I had a thousand tongues I could not say enough.
If I had twenty million fingers I could not write enough.
My love for you is so deep words can't explain how my heart
beats for you. My will is not my own I love you so much Lord
I don't want to do wrong. I've never been in love like this
before.
Cheating is not an option being faithful to you is not a chore.
Because my love is so strong you opened up my heart.
No more bitterness inside.
A love affair is what we have we talk all the time.
You fill me up with overflow and guess what I'm so in love
everyone notices my glow.
When they ask me who I'm in love with I don't waist any time
because I love you so much I don't mind sharing this love so
divine.
Oh what a feeling this love affair I truly have to protect.
The enemy would like it if I walk away so I have to pray.
Pray that you fill me and keep on loving me.
You've opened up my eyes I can see you've always had love for
me.
You are Holy dear and fare.
You are a gentleman I no you care.
How I love this love affair.
So this is my letter to you.
You are the best man I ever had.
This love I have for you no one can ever compare.
I got haters who tell me I love you too much.
But persecution I will bare.
Just to protect this love affair.
So this is my letter to you.

I need thee of Jesus

I need thee oh Lord to keep me
I need thee Father tonight
I need thee Master, Savior, you're my daddy and I need thee
Oh release my promise I need thee
I'm standing on your word order my steps

Oh God I need thee
Oh Lord keep me
I give you my desires and my will I need thee
You're my daddy please strengthen me
I need thee guide me help me stay strong
Oh Jesus I need thee
Take my hand Oh I need thee not my will but your will be done oh
God I need thee
Release what you have promised me

Oh I need thee
I desire what you have for me
Oh yes I do need thee
You are my daddy keep on keeping me
I travail today I need thee I war in my spirit for I need thee
Keep me guide me direct my paths
Order my steps Lord
You are Sovereign I need thee
I don't want my way I want your way I need thee
No mistakes not my way at the end of the day it's you that I need
Oh Jesus yes I need thee

Believe

Would you dare to believe God?
Believe in all that he told you.
Can you stand on his promises?
Believe that God is God all by him self.
Believe that through him you can do all things.
Believe that he is the Father, Son, and Holy Spirit all in one.
Believe that he loves you.
Do you believe that you are here for a purpose?
That's what he has said to you in the secret place that he will
release it to come to pass.

Believe you are not forgotten.
Believe that he rose from the dead on the third day.
Believe you can walk by faith and not by sight.
Believe you are healed. Believe it!
Believe there's promise for your life.
Believe God today love on him stand on his word.
Believe glory to God.
Believe in the dreams he gave you.
Believe I'll say it again believe.
Believe you can live a Holy life.
Believe you will see him again.
Believe that after life there is the judgment.
Believe that Jesus came so that we may have life-life more
abundantly.
Will you believe God today?

Change

Change is on my mind.
It's time for a change it's time for a new start.
I feel change in my spirit I feel my spirit shifting moving forward.
We are going higher in God.

Turning the curve allowing God to lead me and guide me change is here right now.
Change in the atmosphere.
Change in my walk change in my talk.
No more delays no more wondering.
God has released change.

The power of God is in my tongue I speak change I feel change.
I see change in my situation the King of Glory is here I feel him in the air. The sovereign Lord is here.
Abba is here I feel it in my bones.
I see in the spirit its change.
I thank God for change I thank God for the season of Change I don't take it for granted I celebrate the Lord today I worship the Lord.
I magnify the Lord I shabok the Lord I bow down at his feet.
He is a God of change he maneuvers in our life he is the head and not the tail.
Jehovah Jirah my provider Jehovah Nissi my banner I celebrate you.
You are awesome you are God all by yourself.
So today Father it's here it's finally my turn it's my season my destiny has arrived.

Change is here.
Change I will never be the same.
He has changed me.
A new outlook new hope new purpose it's all about change.
Be blessed embrace change.

Fix Me

Fix me Lord
Fix me now
No more playin
No more games
I live for you Lord with no shame
Haters all around on my back
Tellin me the love I have for you is wack

Fix me Lord
Fix me now
I'm a ride or die for you here and now
So I need your love
I need your grace
I get up early just to seek your face
So fix me Lord
Fix me now

I need you Jesus here today
Keep me Lord I got no more play
So down for you is how it is
I'm a soldier in your army
I mean business
So fix me Jesus
Fix me now

The good, the bad, the ugly

Can you see God in all of these things?
Life struggles, disappointments surround me
Stress on the job
Attacks all day long

But I have a question
Can you see God in the good?
When things are going well in your life family has food on the
table
Money in the pocket you can see a movie tonight
You even got enough for a love offering

Can you see God in the bad?
When the roof is leaking no money to be found
Kids asking for lunch money
You need gas in the car

Do you see God in the ugly?
When your wife or your husband disrespect you and don't
come home
And on Sunday morning both of you are in church singing
praise songs.

Do you see God when your friends betray you and stab you in
the back?
Do you see? Do you I ask?
The Good, the Bad, and the ugly God said "see me I'm there
I'm in everything"
I got you even when the attacks come.
See me I'm God I'm in everything

Killing me Softly

You are killing me softly with your words of discouragement
Acting like you my prayer partner all along you are trying to
assassinate my character.

But God ain't having it
You thought I would have died by now
Turn your frown upside down
I'm in the masters hands
He got plans for my life don't get mad get on board it's enough
to go around
So stop talking about me killing me with your tongue

God said touch not my anointed for he gave his son
The Lord said I have to forgive seventy times seventy
God you got to be kidding me.

But for the Lord this I will do
Pray for my enemies
Even though they trying to kill me
To God be the glory!

Lost without you

I am lost without you
Jesus can't think without you
If you ever leave my side where would I be?

No one else can compare with the love you share with me
Oh I'm lost without you
Can't think without you Lord

You are my everything
Can't make a move without you in my life
I believe every word you said
Because today I would be lost without you Jesus

Can't write this poem without you
You are my friend
I'm lost without you Father
Can't breathe without you
I'm lost without your leading
Keep talking to me Jesus I submit my will to you

I'm lost without you

Going all the way

I'm going all the way
I'm going all the way

I'm going all the way with God

No turning back
I'm going all the way

Hold on

Hold on your change is coming
Hold on God will make a way
Hold on God's got your back
Hold on my dear

Your promise is on the way
Hold on God will make a way
Don't give up keep looking to God

Hold on the vision will come to pass
Hold on can't go back
Hold on

Keep standing just hold on your change is coming
Just hold on

Just Sitting

Just sitting here thinking and wondering are you thinking of me
Did you give me back to God?
As I did for you
Did the Lord superimpose me on your spirit?
Did he overwhelm you as of yet?

Just sitting here thinking
Wondering
Do you know who I am?
You seem as you don't have a clue
God told me otherwise
He said you know who I am

Just sitting here wondering do you think of me
God sent me on an assignment just for you
Again I'll say you act like you don't have a clue
I look deep in your eyes and I see you
Why do you act like you don't see me?
Just to let you know the love I have for you is from God above
So no worries on my part I trust in God

So again I say the way the Lord had me to pray
I know he loves you so
But you say you don't know who I am
Baffled is what I am
Are you my perfect fit?
Am I your rib?
These are thoughts that run in my head

Because on today you are in my thoughts
A gentle spirit is what you have

So I just get excited for the love I feel God has for you.
Never in my life have I experienced such a love
So to you my friend in Christ
I wish I could tell you how much God thinks of you
But until the Lord release me to tell you all of this

I will be just sitting here thinking of you!

Promises

God gave me promises and I'm standing on them.
God made me promises and they shall come to pass.
God gave me a promise and I truly believe.
God gave me a promise and its God's seed.
I'm pregnant with a promise can't you see.
God made me a promise that will last eternity

Promises!

I love the Lord

I love the Lord he heard my cry.
After so many tears, and many fears
I love the Lord
I've had head aches, stomach aches, even broke out in hives
But through it all I still love the Lord
Many love lost so many folks walked away but through it all
God had me every step of the way
He saw every tear that fell so many prayers I prayed
wondering did the Lord forget me
Did he know my name?
Even though depression knocked at my door trying to bring a
friend name suicide telling me to stop believing God just give
up and die.

But I must say I love the Lord he heard my cry
Every cry every fear he said I hear you I'm with you my dear
This is your year so don't worry have no fear
Every dream and every promise will come to pass
I'm pre paring you for the future I'm making you ready
You are my chosen vessel I poured the oil on your head
So no more worries no more fears
I'm the Lord your God I'm the one in control
I tried you in the fire I guided you on the path.
So plant your feet and stand fast and open up your ears
Walk in your victory!
I love the Lord no turning back!

Keep me Jesus

Keep me Lord Jesus,
Keep me Lord Jesus,
Keep me Lord Keep me today.
I worship and adore you put no other gods before you
Keep me Lord keep me today
So keep me Lord each and every day
I worship and adore put no other gods before thee
Oh keep me Lord keep me today
Release your glory so I can tell your story oh keep me Lord
keep me today.
You said no more delays' so I stand on your word today.
So shower me with your glory oh keep me today.
I submit my will to you oh yes I do
So keep me Jesus I surrender today
Not my way but order my steps today
So keep me Jesus keep me today.
So this is my prayer this is my song
Keep me Lord all day long
You said I'm going to the nations
I believe you!
Keep me Jesus keep me today.

Thankful

I'm so thankful for you
You changed my life
Now I do things different
Living in sin brought depression
Along with that heartache came
I never thought to drop to my knees to just say help me please
A routine is what is was
I never found happiness in sin just trials and tribulations
Friends came and went they only wanted to be with me for
the moment
Men in and out of my life

Going through the same cycle over and over again.
Still not getting I had no peace within
Until one day I hit rock bottom
No one around all my friends were gone
Including the one I called my true love
There I was all alone
What happened to me I thought to myself.
And then it came to me
God wants me to do some things
He called me one of his own

So yes I'm thankful
Thankful for this day
Thankful that the Lord is using me.

Amen!

Bless your name

I will bless your name
Jesus I will bless your name
From the rising of the sun
I will bless your name
Your name is Holy
I will bless your name

When the bills are over due
I will bless your name
When I don't know what to do
I will bless your name
Trouble on the job
I will bless your name
I will praise you
When my heart is overwhelmed
I shall bless your name
I must bless your name
With my mind body and soul
I will bless your name

Marriage Proposal

Gangsta all day long this is the poem that I write
To God be the Glory
No time for games no time for shame
It's all of me or nothing at all.
You feel me!
It ain't nothing wrong with lovin the gangsta type as long as he
The real deal Holy Field for Christ.
Take all of me or nothing.

I got so much to give
Tired of the counterfeit men all up in my face tryin to live at
my place
The Devil is a liar no more compromising
I ain't having it
I might be feeling you and all of that-but you ain't loving my
number one man.

One two one two I truly wish you could be my boo.
But no telling who you lovin. Straight scared is what I am just
trying to win this race before me.
All the men up in my face trying to live at my place
This is what I say. What do you have to offer me?
I thought you were real but I think you trying to feel me out
no doubt.
No time for games I thought you wanted to change my last
name.
Oh boy what a dang on shame.

Mind blowing this situation surrounding me.
I'm all in the Lord no holding me.
I thought I was worth a man changing. But I guess I was
wrong.

When will Boaz come along?

But no foolishness no not this time.
Life has taught me a real lesson.
Shon keep it stepping.
He don't have no love for you he just preying on you.
Oh God help me please change the words to this poem that I write.
I desire a real man of God I know that's right. Someone to have my back with all the enemies attacks.
I can go on with this.
But the bottom line how did I think he would change my last name. When you keep runnin game.

No Marriage proposal!

Blessed Savior

Jesus blessed savior
You are my keeper my kingsman redeemer
Jesus I desire to please you
Oh how I admire you
To the death of cross you went and then you rose again.
Worship you is what I do
Jesus you are my hero
So many fallen soldiers war on the street people going down
six feet deep.
Afraid to surrender because of what people might think
But Lord give them a chance and show them the way.
You are my blessed savior-have your way
Release your love, release your favor show them your love your
people need you.

Jesus blessed savior your worthy to be praised!
Help the soldiers on the street. Help them not to give up.
It is a way out no doubt you just have to look up to God for
some help.

I know you big pimppin
I know you a thug.
But I got news for you-God has plenty of love
Just repent and ask God to forgive you

Today is your day don't wait
His arms are open wide
Come to Jesus our blessed Savior
He's worthy to be praised!

Waiting

I heard they that wait on the Lord will reap a harvest.
Sometimes in the wait your mind plays tricks on you
Telling you to give up
But the Lord said wait I'll renew your strength.
He will give you wings so you can sour in his kingdom.
So while your waiting stand tall for the Lord.
He has good plans for you.
Stay the course and hold on.
Wait on the Lord
You will reap and not faint
So my dear continue to wait!

My Brother

This is a poem for my brother
I believe in you
Don't give up
Stand your ground
God made you a Priest of your home
A mighty warrior is who you are.

My brother
You stand so strong
You can handle what's going on
God gave you strength
You are made in his own image.
He did not want you to have a blemish.

My brother
You are God's mouth piece
So sound the alarm
My brother
Stand your ground
My brother
Your children need you to show them God's way.

We need you with your integrity
My brother
We need your prayers
I bind up your fears

My brother!

You are needed in God's kingdom
My brother-my brother
All of God's women need you!

Wouldn't it be great?

Wouldn't it be great?
To have my perfect mate
Someone who gets me

Wouldn't it be grand if he was thinking of me during
the course of the day?
Wouldn't it be wonderful to sit together in Sunday service
enjoying life together?

Til death due us part!
Wow!

What would it be like to give someone my heart?
Wouldn't it be great to raise a family and grow old together?
Sitting on a swing holding hands
Wouldn't it be great to finally meet my mate?
The one for me.
Wouldn't it be great to no longer have to search for that
special someone?

Wouldn't it be great if fate would bring us together?

I'm smiling just thinking how great it's going to be
When you and me finally see

Wouldn't it be!

Don't give up

Don't give up
You can dot it
You can make it

Don't give up
Keep on pressin
Don't you dare turn away?

I have to believe I'm going to make it.
Don't give up on your dreams
All the tears was for this time
Don't turn back
Keep on seeking

You can't give up
Oh no you can't
Don't give up
No! No!
You can't quite
You can't quite
Don't give up

Don't give up no matter what continue to stand.

Thank you,

Thank you Father God for pouring into me and showing me that you have a purpose and plan for my life. I want to thank a few people God has blessed me with. Minister Sharon Brown-Bennett (god-mom) thank you for all that you do for me, Minister Talea Jordan (big-sister), V. Imani Bennett (little prayer warrior), Sondra Cartwright (State Mom) Thank you for taking my photo. Dorothy H. Smith (grandmother), Aunt Debbie (I love you), and most of all Mamma (Verdie Brown) thank you for feeding me on Sunday's I love you. And for my praying sisters Minister Christina, Sister Sandy, & Sister Edna, I really love you guys. Peggy I thank you. And I have to thank my dad Michael L. Murray for not leaving me when my mother passed away I really appreciate you I love you very much. And to my BFF Shy you will always be my little girl. A special thank you to Bishop Gilbert Coleman Jr. for pouring into my spirit when you did not even know how much I needed it. And to all of my Brothers and Sisters thank you for praying for me you know who you are. Latanya thank you for being my friend you are a blessing..

Printed in the United States
214703BV00001B/37/P